Table of Contents

For such a seemingly simple dessert, there must be a thousand way to cook fried pies or hand pies, or whatever you choose to call it. We've included a lot of them.

Since most recipes that follow involve the same make dough-and-fry steps once you have cooked the filling, we will cover those below, so they won't need to be repeated throughout the book. If there's some special deviation in the recipe regarding dough-making or frying, that recipe outlines those directions. The fillings in the recipe can still be used with regular pie dough, however, if you choose to opt out of more exotic instructions. Essentially, pie dough is easy to make and even easier to get at the market. To those purists who sniff at buying dough premade or pre-packaged, Nanny would have laughed and said, "Should I still use the old scrub board for the laundry when I have the Maytag?" At some point, good dough is good dough. If it's not quality, don't buy it.

Types of dough used for fried pies:

Refrigerator (usually comes two flat circles to a package)

Freezer (these usually come pressed into a foil pie pan)

Packaged dough (just add water style)

Fillo Dough (we won't use that much, but it's an option)

Biscuits

Bread dough (again, not used here, but it has been done)

Tips for working with traditional pie dough:

Always dip the cutter you are using (glass, can or whatever) in flour before using it to cut out dough for pies.

Pack the dough together into one ball, wrap it in plastic wrap then put it in the fridge for an hour or until it's firm.

When it's ready, flour a flat work area. Roll the dough out with a wooden or glass rolling pin. Cut out wedges of dough for the pies. Our grandmother made hers an oblong shape, similar to McDonald's old hot apple pie. Cut out your desired shapes, then spoon a portion of the apple mixture into the center of each, then fold it over to enclose the filling. Pinch or crimp the edges closed with your fingers or a fork.

Fry as indicated in the frying section that follows. Drain and serve as suggested in the serving section that follows.

BE VERY CAREFUL – Always allow the pie filling to cool somewhat before making the pies. It has been said that active lava flow is hotter than hot pie filling, but the author has never stuck her toe in the volcano to find out while she has been burned by pie filling, so she personally doubts it. Frying is always risky, so be sure to be patient, careful and be conscious during the process.

On frying …

In deep fat fryer or a heavy pan, heat about 3 inches of oil or clarified shortening until boiling. With a spatula, carefully lower pies into the hot oil. Fry until golden brown, turning if necessary, remove the fried pies from the hot oil (be careful – there's a reason they sometimes call them fried hand pies) and then drain the pies on paper towels or napkins.

Traditionally, fried pies are sprinkled with powdered sugar prior to serving – some prefer cinnamon and sugar. In the author's opinion, there is nothing on earth better than vanilla ice cream with fried pies, but some people prefer whipped cream. And it has been said that cheddar cheese is good when served with apple pies, but having never seen this outside of a Dick van Dyke Show episode, we can't comment on that idea.

Modern Traditional Fried Apple Pies

Ingredients:

$\frac{1}{3}$ cup sugar

2 peeled, cored, chopped apples (any apple suitable for a regular pie)

$\frac{1}{2}$ teaspoon ground cinnamon

$\frac{1}{4}$ teaspoon all-spice

2 cups regular, all-purpose flour

1 teaspoon salt

$\frac{1}{2}$ cup Crisco or similar vegetable shortening

$\frac{1}{2}$ cup water

1 cup heated vegetable oil (to fry in)

2 teaspoons powdered sugar (optional)

Directions:

Bring apples, cinnamon and sugar to a boil in a saucepan over low heat. Stir frequently until the apples are soft. At this point, use a big fork or a potato masher to mash the apples into small bits. You want the result to look like apple pie filling, since that's what it is.

Combine flour and salt in a bowl. Add the shortening in with a pastry cutter or large fork until it looks crumbly and mixed in fully with the flour and salt. Gradually stir in the water until dough is moist. Knead dough until the dough bonds together.

Savannah Sunny Fried Peach Pies

Ingredients

Filling
6 ounces dried peaches
1 cup granular sugar
2 cups water
$\frac{1}{4}$ cup butter
$\frac{1}{2}$ teaspoon cinnamon

Dough
2 cups all-purpose flour
1 teaspoon salt
$\frac{1}{2}$ cup vegetable shortening
$\frac{1}{2}$ cup of milk

Instructions

Fill a pan with water, place the dried fruit in the water and bring it to a boil. Reduce flame and let the pan simmer until the fruit looks more like cooked fruit and less like dried. Add the rest of the ingredients and then mash them with a large fork or a masher.

See the dough and frying section at the front of the book for the next steps.

Big Easy Apple Raisin Fried Pies

Ingredients:

$^1/_2$ cup sugar

2 peeled, cored, chopped apples

$^1/_2$ cup raisins

$^1/_2$ cup good bourbon

3 pounds (about a dozen) Granny Smith apples

$^1/_2$ teaspoon ground cinnamon

2 cups regular, all-purpose flour

1 teaspoon salt

$^1/_4$ teaspoon all-spice

$^1/_2$ cup Crisco or similar vegetable shortening

$^1/_2$ cup water

1 cup heated vegetable oil (to fry in)

2 teaspoons powdered sugar (optional)

Directions:

Bring apples, cinnamon and sugar to a boil in a saucepan over low heat. Stir frequently until the apples are soft. At this point, use a big fork or a potato masher to mash the apples into small bits. You want the result to look like apple pie filling, since that's what it is.

See the dough and frying section at the front of the book for the next steps. These particular fried pies taste great in cinnamon and sugar.

Easy Biscuit Apricot Pies

Ingredients:

A dozen or so of those Grands-style layered biscuits

6-7 ounces dried apricots

1 cup sugar

2 cups water

$\frac{1}{4}$ cup butter

$\frac{1}{2}$ teaspoon cinnamon

Directions:

Fill a saucepan with water, place the dried fruit in the water and bring it to a boil. Reduce flame and let the pan simmer until the fruit looks more like cooked fruit and less like dried. Add the rest of the ingredients and then mash them with a large fork or a masher.

Press the biscuit out into a large circle. Carefully add some of the apricot mixture into the middle of each circle, then fold over and pinch the edges with a fork (or your fingers if the apricot filling isn't too hot).

Heat oil in heavy saucepan. Use a spatula to carefully place the little pies into the hot oil. Fry until crispy and brown. Remove them to some napkins or paper towels to drain excess oil.

Boysenberry Fried Pies

Ingredients:

Filling:

1 cup of water + $\frac{1}{4}$ cup of water

$\frac{2}{3}$ cup of granulated sugar

Pinch of salt

1 tablespoon corn syrup

3 tablespoons cornstarch

1 teaspoon lemon juice

1 16 oz bag of frozen boysenberries or a comparable amount of fresh

2 crust pie shells (or your own dough recipe, prepared)

Directions:

In a saucepan, combine water, sugar, salt, corn syrup and lemon juice and bring them to a boil. In a mixing bowl, blend cornstarch, boysenberries and water. Making sure they're well-blended, add the saucepan contents into the boysenberry mixture. If needed, you may thicken the filling with more cornstarch.

Unfold dough from package. Place both circles on a floured surface. Cut out the desired shapes, spoon boysenberry filling in the center, then fold over, enclosing the filling inside. Crimp the edges with a fork or (being careful!) your fingers. As always, powdered sugar, if you like. Ice cream is also nice.

Old-Fashioned Hot Kitchen Blueberry Fried Pies

Ingredients:
Dough:
2 cups of flour
$\frac{1}{2}$ teaspoon salt
$\frac{1}{2}$ cup of chilled lard
$\frac{1}{4}$ cup of cold water

Filling:
2 cups of fresh or frozen blueberries
$\frac{1}{2}$ cup of sugar
3 tablespoons of flour
1 teaspoon of lemon juice
$\frac{1}{2}$ teaspoon of cinnamon
$\frac{1}{2}$ cup of water

Directions:
Prepare the dough. Once your dough is chilling, combine all ingredients into a saucepan. Bring it to boil over medium heat for a few minutes.

Spoon filling into the center of each pre-cut piece of dough. Fold over the crust, sealing the filling inside, then pinch the edges closed with a fork or your fingers. See the dough and frying section at the front of the book for the next steps.

Quickie Crisp Pies

This is the fast-and-dirty version of fried pies. It's incredibly easy and very basic. It involves a package of refrigerator pie crusts and a big can of any kind of pie filling – any kind. Just remember to leave room around the pie filling for a good seal.

See <u>the dough and frying section</u> at the front of the book for the next steps.

Fried Dried Apple Biscuit Hand Pies

Ingredients:

8 ounces dried apples

1 cup water

$\frac{1}{3}$ cup sugar

1 tablespoon butter

1 can flake-like refrigerated biscuits

vegetable oil, for frying

Directions:

Combine apples and water in saucepan; bring to a boil. Cover, reduce heat, and simmer for 30 or until soft and mashable. Turn off heat, allow to cool and then use a large fork or potato masher to further pulp the cooked apples. Fold in the sugar and butter and mix.

Place each biscuit on a lightly floured surface. Smash it out into the right size (put two or more together if you like larger pies). Place a tablespoon of apple mixture on half of each biscuit, fold over to cover the apple filling, then press the biscuit edges together with a fork or your fingers (be careful, it's hot). See the dough and frying section at the front of the book for the next steps. Makes about a dozen pies.

Nanny's Dried and Fried Fruit Pies (Whatever fruit or fruits you like)

Dough:

1 teaspoon salt

1 cup Crisco or other good vegetable shortening

1 beaten egg

$\frac{1}{4}$ cup cold water

1 teaspoon white vinegar

Mix together flour and salt. Mix in the shortening until the mixture looks crumbly. Stir beaten egg together with water then add to dough base. Add in the vinegar, mixing just enough until everything is combined. Plastic wrap the dough and refrigerate it for an hour or so.

Filling:

Each cup of dried fruit requires $\frac{1}{2}$ cup of water and two tablespoons of sugar. You may need to increase or decrease this based on the fruit you use.

3 cups dried fruit

1 $\frac{1}{2}$ cups water

6 tablespoons sugar

$\frac{1}{4}$ teaspoon cinnamon

$\frac{1}{4}$ teaspoon all-spice

On low heat, cook the dried fruit until soft, about 30 minutes or so (time will vary according to the fruit used). With a potato masher or big fork, mash the fruit up and mix in sugar, cinnamon and all-spice. See dough and frying section for the next steps.

Chocolate Fried Pies

Ingredients